Party Cupcakes

SHEREEN VAN BALLEGOOYEN

Party Cupcakes

For my beautiful girls, Amber and Hayley, my sunshines.
For Garth, my everything. x

First published 2013 by
Guild of Master Craftsman Publications Ltd
Castle Place, 166 High Street, Lewes,
East Sussex BN7 1XU

Text © Shereen van Ballegooyen, 2013
Copyright in the Work © GMC Publications Ltd, 2013

ISBN 978 1 86108 985 4

A catalogue record for this book is available from the
British Library.

Publisher: Jonathan Bailey
Production Manager: Jim Bulley
Managing Editor: Gerrie Purcell
Senior Project Editor: Wendy McAngus
Editor: Cath Senker
Managing Art Editor: Gilda Pacitti
Designer: Ginny Zeal
Photography: Anthony Bailey and Gilda Pacitti

Set in Gill Sans
Colour origination by GMC Reprographics
Printed and bound in China

Why we love party cupcakes

Welcome to my Party Cupcakes book. This book is filled with 30 delightful, fun cupcake projects. My customers know me for the little details in my work so I have made up these projects using as many techniques as possible. They will show you step by step how to create your very own perfect party cupcakes.

The projects in this book cover parties for girls, for boys and for adults too. I love colour, and I have used bright colours here so that your cupcakes will stand out from the crowd and brighten up any party table.

Shereen van Ballegooyen

Contents

25

26

27

28

29

30

This cute little cow gives you the opportunity to try your hand at painting on a cupcake. With her sweet-natured face she will make the perfect addition to any party.

Cute cow

You will need

White modelling paste

Small ball tool

Sugar glue

2 x ⅙in (4mm) black sugar balls

Brown modelling paste

Craft knife

Small daisy cutter

Fine paintbrush

Dark brown paste colour

A little clear alcohol or rejuvenator spirit

Large blossom plunger cutter

Orange modelling paste

1 x ⅓in (8mm) yellow sugar pearl

Medium blossom plunger cutter

Blue modelling paste

1 x ⅙in (4mm) pink sugar ball

Bright green modelling paste (mix melon and party green paste colour)

Bright green sugarpaste

Cupcake (see page 138)

Shell tool

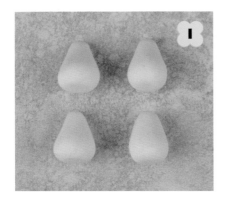

1 Legs Using the white modelling paste, roll and shape 4 cone-shaped pieces to make the legs.

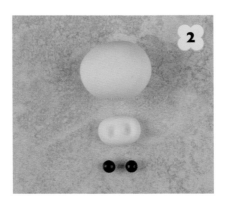

2 Head Roll a ball and make it into a slight oval shape for the head. Roll a smaller oval shape for the nostrils. Make the nostrils with the small ball tool.

3 Body Roll a ball and shape it into an oval, pressing the front of the shape with your thumb to make an indent for the head to settle on.

4 Assemble Use the sugar glue to glue the body to the legs and stick the head to the body on the indented side. Glue on 2 black sugar balls for eyes.

5 Ears (make 2) Roll a teardrop shape from white modelling paste, press it flat and then trim the bottom so you have a triangular shape.

6 Horns and fringe With the brown modelling paste, roll a little sausage with pointed ends and bend slightly. Cut out a small daisy with the daisy cutter for the fringe of hair.

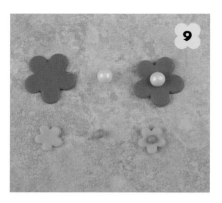

7 **Tail** With brown modelling paste, roll a long teardrop shape and flatten the larger side slightly. Cut into the flat piece with the craft knife to make 'hair' on the tail.

8 **Assemble** Add the ears, then the horns between the ears and the fringe on top of the horns. Use a fine paintbrush, dark brown paste colour and a little rejuvenator spirit or clear alcohol to paint patches.

9 **Flowers** Cut a large orange blossom with the large blossom plunger cutter and finish off with a yellow pearl. Cut a smaller blue flower with the medium blossom plunger cutter and finish with a small pink sugar ball.

10 **Finish off** Cover the cupcake with bright green sugarpaste (see page 142) and use the shell tool to scratch this icing for a grass-effect finish. Finish off your project by adding the cow and the little flowers to the cupcake.

This delightful little flower girl perched happily on a bright, frilly flower is 100 per cent girly and is sure to prove a huge hit at any little girl's party.

Flower girl

You will need

Dark pink modelling paste

Small ball tool

Flesh pink modelling paste (mix chestnut with cream paste colour)

Craft knife

Scallop tool

2 × black nonpareils

Yellow flower/petal paste

Large 5-petal cutter

Foam drying sheet

Sugar glue

Large daisy-centre stamp

White modelling paste

Piece of uncooked spaghetti for support

Dark brown modelling paste

A little vegetable fat

Dark green sugarpaste

Cupcake (see page 138)

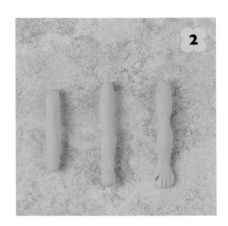

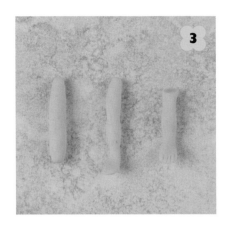

1 Dress With dark pink modelling paste, roll a ball and shape it into a rounded cone. Press around the bottom of the dress to flatten it a bit. Use a small ball tool to make 2 little holes for the legs to fit under the dress.

2 Arms and hands (make 2) With flesh pink modelling paste, roll a sausage shape. Use your fingers to indent in the middle for the elbow and the wrist. Use a craft knife to mark the fingers (see page 146).

3 Legs and feet (make 2) Roll a sausage shape. Use your fingers to indent the middle for the knee and then shape the foot at the bottom. Use a craft knife to mark toes and trim the top of the leg.

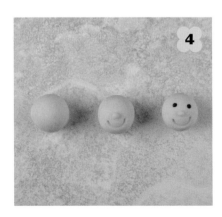

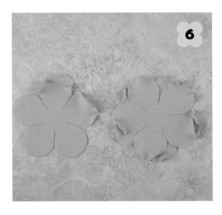

4 Face Roll a ball for the face. Make a smile with the scallop tool. Shape a nose and add black nonpareils for eyes.

5 Flower Roll out some yellow flower paste and cut out 2 large 5-petal flowers with the 5-petal cutter.

6 Flaring Flare the petals on the flowers (see page 148) on the foam drying sheet. Overlap the flowers to glue them so you can see all the petals.

7 **Centre** Use white modelling paste and a large daisy-centre stamp to create a centre for your flower. Attach with a little sugar glue.

8 **Assemble** Add the legs under the dress. Add the arms. Push a piece of spaghetti down into the top of the body and press the head gently into position on top. Using some dark brown modelling paste mixed with vegetable fat, add the flower girl's hair (see hair technique on page 147).

9 **Finish off** Cover the cupcake with dark green sugarpaste (see page 142). Stick the large frilly flower to the cupcake and then stick the flower girl on top of the flower.

Having a sea-themed party? Well this little guy is all tentacles and smiley face – just the thing for your little one's birthday-party table.

Otto the octopus

You will need

Bright green modelling paste (mix melon and party green paste colour)

Craft knife

Small and very small circle cutters

White modelling paste

Light blue modelling paste

Sugar glue

2 x ⅙in (4mm) black sugar balls

Lighter bright green modelling paste

Scallop tool

Black edible-ink pen

Cupcake (see page 138)

Blue sugarpaste

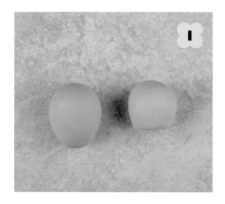

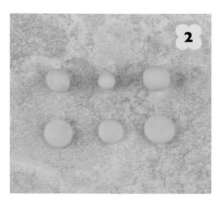

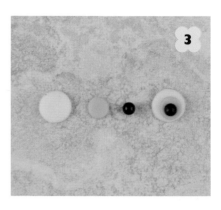

1 Body Roll a ball from bright green modelling paste and shape into an oval. Trim the bottom with a craft knife.

2 Head spots With the lighter bright green modelling paste, roll some balls and press them flat to make spots for the octopus's head.

3 Eyes Cut out 2 small white circles and 2 very small light blue circles. Stick the blue circles onto the white circles with sugar glue. Glue a black sugar ball onto each eye.

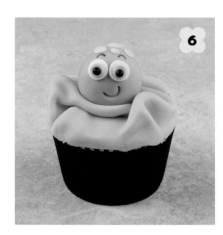

4 Face Make a smile with a scallop tool. Add the eyes. Draw on eyebrows with black edible-ink pen and add the spots to the top of the head.

5 Water Cover your cupcake with blue sugarpaste to create the water effect (see page 144).

6 Assemble Add the head to the middle of the cupcake.

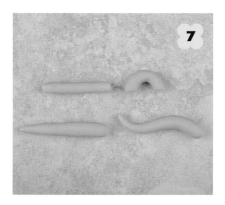

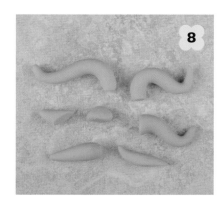

7 **Tentacles** Roll out a sausage shape in bright green modelling paste. Fold over and trim the bottom for an arched shape. To make longer tentacles, roll out long teardrop shapes and bend, curl and twist them.

8 **Shapes and sizes** Make 8 tentacles altogether, in a variety of shapes and sizes. You can make some of the tentacles in 2 parts to give the effect of going in and out of the water.

9 **Assemble** Build the octopus on the cupcake, pressing the tentacles in between the 'waves' so that it looks like the octopus is in the water.

10 **Finish off** Add all the tentacles to finish off the cupcake.

This perfect little pink pig with a dainty flower,
playing in her own chocolate buttercream mud puddle,
is bound to delight the guests at any animal-themed party.

Little pig

You will need

Light pink modelling paste

Craft knife

Large ball tool

Small ball tool

Sugar glue

2 × ⅙in (4mm) black sugar balls

Large blossom cutter and veiner set

Dark yellow modelling paste

1 green ⅓in (8mm) sugar pearl

Bright green sugarpaste

Cupcake (see page 138)

A teaspoon of chocolate buttercream (see page 140)

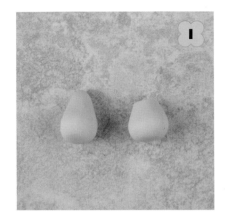

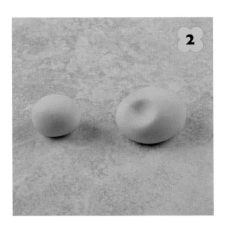

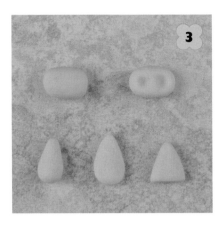

1 **Legs** With light pink modelling paste, roll 4 little cone-shaped legs and trim off the tops with a craft knife.

2 **Head and body** Roll a small ball for the head and a larger oval shape for the body. Use a large ball tool to make an indent in the top of the body.

3 **Features** For the nose, roll an oval shape and use a small ball tool to make the nostrils. For the ears, roll 2 teardrop shapes, press them flat, then trim off the bottom.

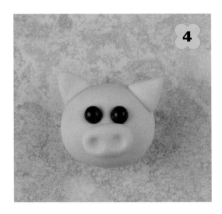

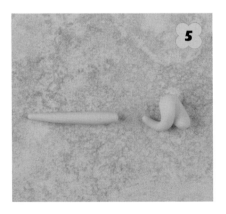

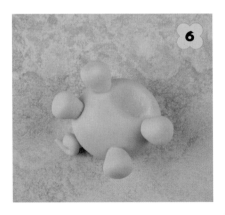

4 **Face** Assemble the face by adding black sugar balls for the eyes and attaching the nostrils and ears with sugar glue.

5 **Tail** Roll a long, thin teardrop shape and twist it to make a curly tail.

6 **Assemble** Add the tail to the bottom of the body. Add the legs to the top of the body, on the belly.

7 **Assemble** Attach the head to the indent on the body.

8 **Flower** Use the large blossom cutter and veiner to make a flower with dark yellow modelling paste. Finish off with a green sugar pearl.

9 **Finish off** Cover the cupcake with bright green sugarpaste (see page 142). Add a smudge of chocolate buttercream on top and lay the pig on top of that. Add the flower.

This little dinosaur is a unique character who can be made in any colour to suit your party theme. He's a bright and cheerful creature who will make little children grin from ear to ear.

Dotty dinosaur

You will need

Medium blue modelling paste

Small round cookie cutter (scalloped side)

Small ball tool

White modelling paste

2 × ⅙in (4mm) black sugar balls

2 smallest sizes of round cookie cutters

Light blue modelling paste

Craft knife

Sugar glue

Black edible-ink pen

Bright green sugarpaste

Cupcake (see page 138)

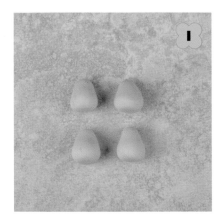

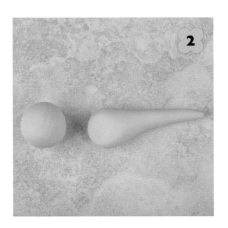

1 **Legs** Using some medium blue modelling paste, roll 4 little cone shapes for legs and flatten the tops a little.

2 **Head, body and tail** Roll a ball for the head. For the body, roll a big teardrop shape with a long, thin tail.

3 **Assemble** Attach the body to the legs and curl the tail up a little at the end.

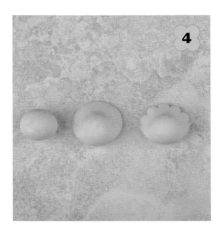

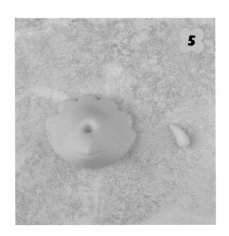

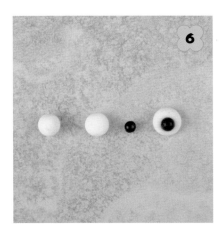

4 **Head** Roll a ball and press the edges and top of the face flat. Use the scalloped side of a small cookie cutter to cut around the top of the head.

5 **Horn** With the ball tool, make a small hole in the face for the horn to go. Roll a small horn using a little light blue paste.

6 **Eyes** Roll 2 small white balls, press them flat and attach black sugar balls for the eyes.

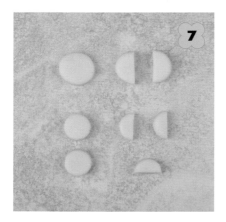

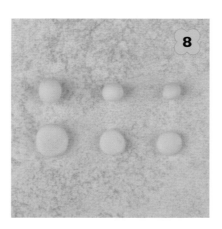

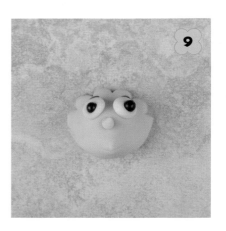

7 **Spine plates** With the circle cutters, cut 1 medium and 2 small circles from light blue paste and use the craft knife to cut them all in half.

8 **Body spots** Roll out some balls from light blue modelling paste for the spots on the dinosaur's body and press them flat.

9 **Face** Stick the eyes and the horn to the face with the sugar glue and draw on some eyebrows with black edible-ink pen.

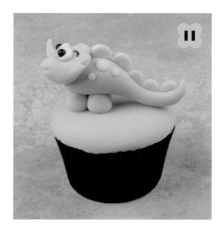

10 **Assemble** Fit the head to the body and the plates up along the tail and spine. Add the little spots on the back.

11 **Finish off** Cover the cupcake in bright green sugarpaste (see page 142). Add the completed dinosaur to your cupcake.

These pretty cupcakes can be adjusted and used for any occasion at all. Add special messages with your clear stamps or pretty pictures to add a personal touch to these lovely little cakes.

Celebration

You will need

2 circle cutters of your choice, one smaller than the other

Dark purple modelling paste

⅙in (4mm) small round cookie cutter

White modelling paste

Clear stamp of your choice

Sugar glue

Petunia cutter and veiner set

⅓in (8mm) sugar pearls – 2 white and 1 purple

Green modelling paste

Heart cutter

Primrose cutter

Large blossom cutter and veiner

Buttercream for piping

White sugarpaste

Cupcake (see page 138)

1 Disks Use the scallop side of the medium round cookie cutter to cut a dark purple disk. Use the round side of the small round cookie cutter to cut a white disk. These disks should be about ⅙in (4mm) thick.

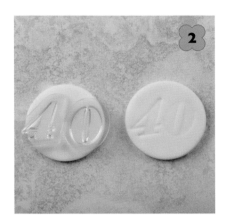

2 Imprint Select a clear stamp to imprint your white disk.

3 Assemble With sugar glue, stick the white disk with the print onto the bigger purple disk.

4 Petunia Use the petunia cutter and veiner to create a purple flower and finish off with a white sugar pearl.

5 Leaf Make up a green leaf using the heart cutter (see page 151).

6 Primrose Cut out a primrose with the primrose cutter and finish off with a white sugar pearl.

7 **Large blossom** Using the large blossom cutter and veiner, create a flower and finish off with a purple sugar pearl.

8 **Assemble** Make buttercream (see page 140). Cover the cupcake with white sugarpaste (see page 142) and pipe a swirl of buttercream on top.

9 **Decorate** Add the decorations to your cupcake.

This fluffy, bashful-looking sheep has her own meadow and flowers and will complete any party table. Why not make the little pig and the cute cow (see pages 22–5 and 10–13) to accompany her?

Shy sheep

You will need

Black modelling paste
White modelling paste
Small circle cutter
2 × black ⅙in (4mm) sugar balls
Small ball tool
Medium blossom plunger cutter

Blue modelling paste
3 × pink ⅙in (4mm) sugar balls
Shell tool
Dark green sugarpaste
Cupcake (see page 138)

1 Legs With black modelling paste, roll 4 little cone shapes for the legs

2 Body With white modelling paste, roll a large ball for the body. With the small circle cutter, make imprints on the body to give a wool effect.

3 Head Roll a black oval shape and flatten the top of the face slightly, leaving the bottom of the face rounded.

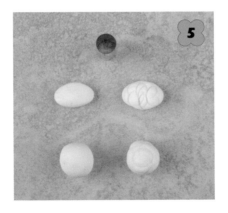

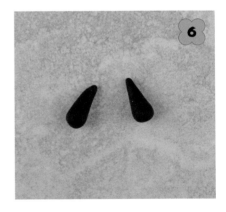

4 Face Roll 2 small white balls and press them flat. Add black sugar balls for eyes. Add the eyes to the top part of the face. Use a small ball tool to make the nostrils.

5 Fringe and tail Roll a white oval for the fringe and then a small white ball for the tail. Use the small circle cutter to make a wool effect on both.

6 Ears Roll 2 small black teardrop shapes for the ears.

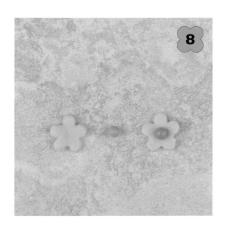

7 Assemble Attach the legs to the body and stick the face to the front of the body with sugar glue. Add the fringe, ears and tail.

8 Flower (make 3) Cut a small blue flower with the medium blossom plunger cutter and finish off with a pink sugar ball.

9 Finish off Cover the cupcake with dark green sugarpaste (see page 142). Use a shell tool to 'scratch' on the sugarpaste on the top of the cupcake to give a grass effect (see page 147). Add the sheep and the flowers on top.

Holding a pretty party for a budding ballerina? These perfect ballet pumps and beautiful flowers are sure to make your little dancer and friends pirouette with joy.

Ballet bouquet

You will need

Medium pink modelling paste

Leaf- and flower-shaping tool

Craft knife

Tiny details mould

Sugar glue

Petunia cutter and veiner set

Pale pink modelling paste

3 x ⅓in (8mm) sugar pearls

Small 5-petal cutter

Medium daisy centre stamp

White modelling paste

Light green modelling paste

Small sunflower plunger cutter

Medium daisy cutter

Primrose cutter

Heart cutter

Dark pink sugarpaste

Cupcake (see page 138)

Buttercream for piping

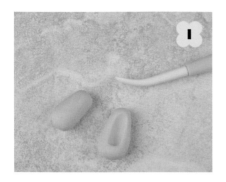

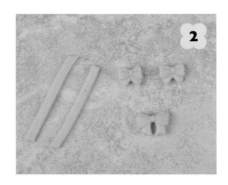

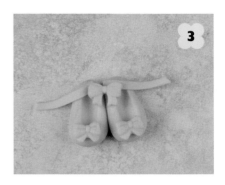

1 **Shoes (make 2)** Using medium pink modelling paste, roll a shoe shape, a little fatter at one end. Using the leaf- and flower-shaping tool, make an indent for the opening of the shoe.

2 **Straps and bows** With the craft knife, cut 2 thin strips for the shoe straps. Using the tiny details mould, make 1 medium and 2 small bows.

3 **Completing the shoes** With the sugar glue, glue the inside backs of the shoes together. Glue on the straps. Add a little bow to the front of each shoe and the medium bow to the middle at the back.

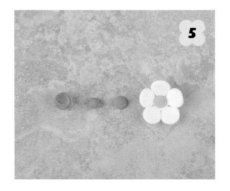

4 **Embossed flower** Use the petunia cutter and veiner to create a pale pink petunia and finish with a white sugar pearl.

5 **Simple flower** Using a small 5-petal cutter, cut a white flower and use a medium daisy centre stamp to create a pink centre.

6 **Pretty daisy** With the small sunflower plunger cutter, cut out 2 flowers. Use the medium daisy cutter to cut out 2 daisies in medium pink. Using sugar glue stick the flowers together, overlapping so you can see all the petals. Add a sugar pearl to finish.

Tip

Tip
Decorate lots of cakes in many different colours so that your party guests can pick one to match their outfits.

7 Primrose Cut a white flower with the primrose cutter and finish with a white sugar pearl. Make a leaf from pale green modelling paste, using the heart cutter (see page 151).

8 Cupcake Cover your cupcake with dark pink sugarpaste (see page 142) and add a swirl of buttercream (see page 140).

9 Decorate Add the ballet shoes and all the flowers to the cupcake.

This charming monkey sitting on a cupcake
would make any birthday girl or boy smile. This is a lovely
little cupcake for a jungle- or animal-themed party.

Cheeky monkey

You will need

Dark brown modelling paste

Light brown modelling paste

Heart cutter

Craft knife

Scallop tool

Ball tool

2 x ⅙in (4mm) black sugar balls

Sugar glue

Piece of uncooked spaghetti for support

Petunia cutter and veiner set

Light pink modelling paste

1 x ⅓in (8mm) white sugar pearl

Leaf cutter

Dark green sugarpaste

Cupcake (see page 138)

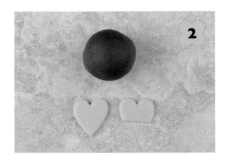

1 **Body** Roll a ball from dark brown modelling paste and form it into a rounded cone shape for the belly, the fatter part at the bottom and the narrower part at the top.

2 **Head** Roll a ball for the head. For the eyes, roll out some light brown modelling paste, cut a heart shape with the heart cutter and trim off the bottom of the heart with the craft knife.

3 **Lower part of face** Make an oval shape and flatten the top half a little, leaving the bottom part rounded. Use the scallop tool to make a smile and the ball tool to create nostrils.

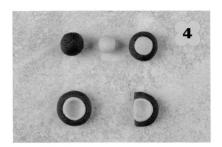

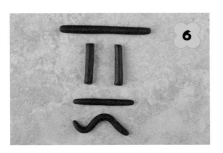

4 **Ears (make 2)** Roll a dark brown ball and a smaller light brown ball, and put the light brown ball on top of the dark brown one. Use the ball tool to press the 2 balls together and then trim off a piece at the side.

5 **Assemble head** With sugar glue, stick on the 2 black sugar balls for eyes, the lower part of the face and the ears on the side of the head.

6 **Arms, legs and tail** Roll a long sausage shape with dark brown modelling paste and cut it into 2. Repeat this to make 2 arms and 2 legs. Roll another sausage shape for the tail and bend and shape it.

7 **Hands, belly and feet (make 2 hands, 1 belly and 2 feet)** With light brown paste, roll an oval to make a hand and make indents for the fingers with the craft knife. Roll a teardrop shape and press flat for the belly. Roll another oval to make a foot, flatten slightly and make indents for the toes. Attach the hands and feet to the arms and legs respectively.

8 **Assemble** Push a piece of uncooked spaghetti through the body and add the head to the top for support. Add the belly and then the legs, arms and tail with sugar glue.

9 **Flower** Use the petunia cutter and veiner to make a light pink flower. Finish off with a white sugar pearl.

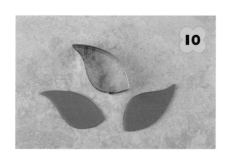

10 **Leaf** Use a leaf cutter and dark green modelling paste to make 2 leaves. Cut them just before putting your cupcake together so you can bend and shape the leaves directly on the cupcake.

11 **Finish off** Cover the cupcake with dark green sugarpaste (see page 142). Put the monkey on top, with the leaves on the side of the cupcake and the flower on the leaves.

This mini pirate will brighten up any swashbuckling party table. Make longer hair or paint pink stripes to make a girl version of this fun cupcake.

Mini pirate

You will need

Dark brown modelling paste

Black modelling paste

Craft knife

White modelling paste

Small ball tool

Red paste colour

Fine paintbrush

Waistcoat template (see page 152)

Flesh pink modelling paste (mix chestnut with cream paste colour)

Scallop tool

Small circle cutter

1 black nonpareil

Black edible-ink pen

Sugar glue

Rejuvenator spirit or clear alcohol for painting

Piece of uncooked spaghetti for support

A little vegetable fat

Sugarcraft gun with grass/hair disk

Beach-coloured sugarpaste

Cupcake (see page 138)

Marbled modelling paste from white, grey and black paste
   (see Moon rocket, pages 102–5)

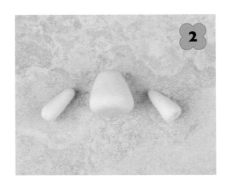

1 Trouser and shoes Roll a sausage shape with dark brown paste and fold it in half to make trouser legs. Trim the bottom of the legs with the craft knife. With black modelling paste, roll 2 ovals for the feet.

2 Sleeves and body Roll out 2 teardrop shapes from white modelling paste and flatten the ends to form the sleeves. Make holes for the hands in the end of the sleeves with a small ball tool. Shape a triangular body.

3 Assemble Add the body to the trousers and the shoes to the end of the trousers. Using the paintbrush and red paste, paint some red stripes on the front of the body.

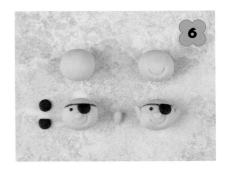

4 Waistcoat and hands Cut a waistcoat from black modelling paste using the template on page 152. To shape the hands, roll a ball from flesh pink modelling paste and make a teardrop shape. Press flat and cut out a 'v' for the thumb (see page 146). Roll wrists at the base of the hands.

5 Assemble Add the waistcoat and sleeves. Use some rejuvenator spirit or clear alcohol with the red paste colour to paint stripes on the pirate's sweater. Push the piece of uncooked spaghetti through the pirate's body to attach the head to.

6 Face Roll a ball and use the scallop tool to add a smile. Shape a nose and attach. Cut a small black circle with the cutter and trim to make the eye patch. Position it and draw the strap with the black pen. Add a black nonpareil for the other eye. Make teardrop-shaped ears and attach with sugar glue.

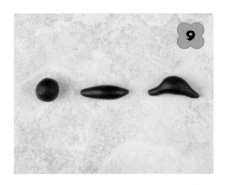

7 Assemble Add the head to the piece of spaghetti. Attach the hands to the sleeves.

8 Hair Add the hair to the pirate's head using the technique on page 147.

9 Hat Roll a ball from black modelling paste and shape into a hat with narrow ends and a wider part in the middle.

10 Finish off Cover the cupcake with caramel-coloured sugarpaste (see page 142). Stick the hat to the pirate's head and add him to the cupcake. Mix black, white and grey paste to create a marble effect and roll into balls to make stones.

This hilarious hippo is having a lazy day lounging in some cool water in the African sun. She will add lots of character to the table of a jungle-themed party.

Happy hippo

You will need

Grey modelling paste
Cone tool
Craft knife
White modelling paste
Blue sugarpaste
Ball tool

Scallop tool
2 x ⅙in (4mm) black sugar balls
Sugar glue
Black edible-ink pen
Cupcake (see page 138)

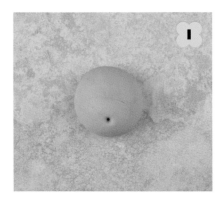

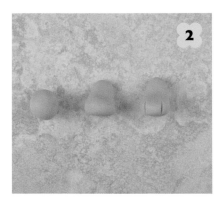

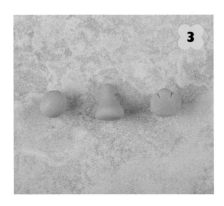

1 **Body** Form the belly from grey modelling paste by rolling a ball and then pressing flat with your palm to give a nice rounded tummy. Use a cone tool to make a little belly button.

2 **Back legs (make 2)** Roll a ball and then shape into a leg and foot. Use a craft knife to indent little toes on the foot. The back legs are slightly longer than the front.

3 **Front legs (make 2)** Roll a ball, then shape the leg and foot. Make the top of one leg teardrop shaped so it will drape onto the belly. Trim the top of the other so that it will face up.

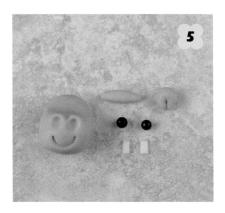

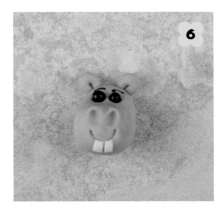

4 **Face** Roll a ball and shape the face with the snout coming out at the front. The top of the face where the eyes will go is quite flat.

5 **Features** Make nostrils with the ball tool and the mouth with the scallop tool. Roll and fold the ears into shape and cut 2 little white teeth from white modelling paste. Use 2 black sugar balls for eyes.

6 **Finishing the face** Trim the bottom of the ears to fit better on the head, and attach them. Add the eyes and teeth to the face with a little sugar glue. Draw on eyebrows with black edible-ink pen.

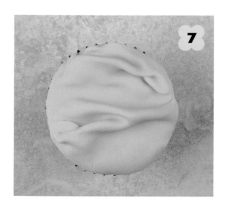

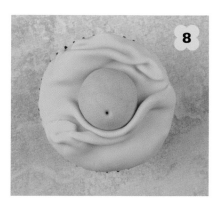

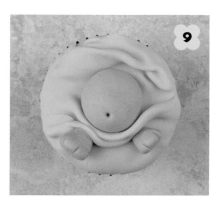

7 Water Cover your cupcake with blue sugarpaste to give a water effect (see page 144).

8 Belly Sugar-glue the belly onto the cupcake while the 'water' is still soft, so you can manipulate the sugarpaste to fit neatly around the belly.

9 Legs Add the back legs to the bottom of the belly, once again while the sugarpaste 'water' is still soft so you can tuck them in easily.

10 Finish Add the front legs and face to the hippo. Wrap the one little leg that has a teardrop shape at the top over the belly slightly.

Need a token for Valentine's Day or just want to say 'I love you'?
This heart design is simple to put together to impress your loved one.
It's also perfect for an engagement party or wedding anniversary.

Love hearts

You will need

White modelling paste

Red modelling paste

Red sugarpaste

Lace texture mat (or mat of your choice)

Large and medium heart cutters

Tiny details silicone mould

Sugar glue

Red sugarpaste

Cupcake (see page 138)

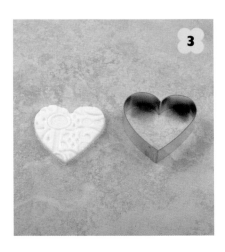

1 **Rolling** Roll out white modelling paste to about ⅛in (5mm) thick.

2 **Embossing** Use an embossing mat to imprint on the paste. I used a lace mat.

3 **White heart** Cut out a large heart from the embossed paste.

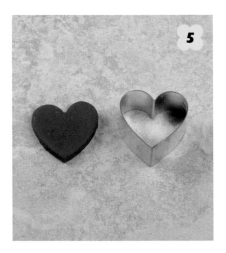

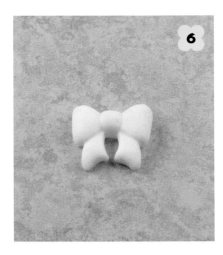

4 **Rolling** Roll out red paste to about ⅛in (5mm) thick.

5 **Red heart** Cut out a medium red heart.

6 **Bow** Use the tiny details mould to press out a large bow from white paste.

7 **Assemble** Sugar-glue the red heart to the white heart with sugar glue and add the bow on top.

8 **Finish off** Cover the cupcake with red sugarpaste (see page 142). Add the stacked heart to your cupcake.

Tip
Try this decoration in various colours for different effects – pink for a softer feel or a black background for something more dramatic. Leave the bow off the decoration for a simpler, understated look.

This cheerful little zebra in her own little field with flowers is great for safari-themed parties. You'll need to carefully hand paint the stripes.

Zany zebra

You will need:

White modelling paste

2 x ⅙in (4mm) black balls

Craft knife

Black edible-ink pen

Sugar glue

Small ball tool

Scallop tool

Fine paintbrush

Rejuvenator spirit or clear alcohol

Black paste colour

Bright green modelling paste (mix a little melon with party green paste colour)

Heart cutter

Large blossom cutter and veiner set

Yellow modelling paste

1 x ⅓in (8mm) green sugar pearl

Dark green sugarpaste

Cupcake (see page 138)

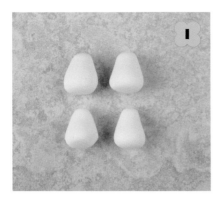

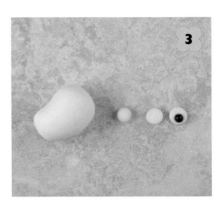

1 **Legs** Roll and shape 4 cone-shaped legs from white modelling paste. Slightly flatten the tops.

2 **Body** Start with a large ball and then shape an oval body. Use your thumb to flatten the top for the head to sit on.

3 **Head and features** Roll a ball for the head, shaping the front a little longer for the snout. To make the eyes, roll a ball, press it flat and attach a black sugar ball.

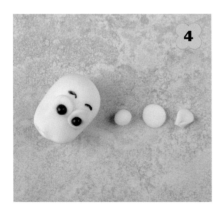

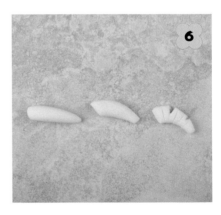

4 **Face** Add the eyes to the face. To make each ear, make a ball, press it flat and fold it over. Trim the bottom of the ear with the craft knife so it sticks more easily to the head. Draw on eyebrows with black edible-ink pen.

5 **Assemble** Stick the body to the legs and the head to the body with sugar glue. Add the ears. Use a small ball tool to make nostrils and a scallop tool to make a little smile on the side of the zebra's face.

6 **Mane** Roll a teardrop shape, flatten it slightly and trim the front to make a sharp finish. Use the craft knife to cut some 'v' shapes into the mane and make some lines.

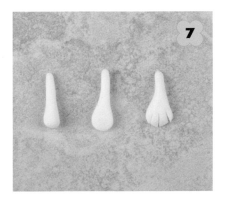

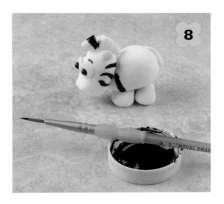

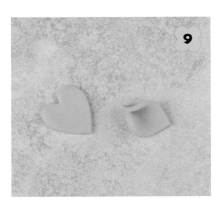

7 **Tail** Roll a teardrop shape, press the larger end flat and cut some lines into the flat part of the tail.

8 **Paint** Sugar-glue on the mane and tail. Use the paintbrush with a little rejuvenator spirit or clear alcohol and black paste colour to paint on the stripes. Leave to dry.

9 **Leaf** With bright green modelling paste, use the heart cutter to make up a leaf (see page 151).

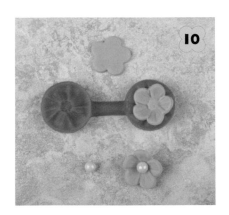

10 **Embossed blossom** Using the large blossom cutter and veiner and yellow modelling paste make up a flower. Finish it off with a green sugar pearl.

11 **Finish off** Cover the cupcake with dark green sugarpaste (see page 142). Add the zebra, flower and leaf to the cupcake.

This awesome little astronaut is perfect for a space-themed party. Add him to his moon-effect cupcake to create a full space theme with remarkably little effort.

Ace astronaut

You will need:

White modelling paste

Craft knife

Black edible-ink pen

Circle cutter

Black modelling paste

Grey, black and white sugarpaste combined to give
slightly marbled effect (see Moon rocket, pages 102–5)

Cupcake (see page 138)

Ball tool

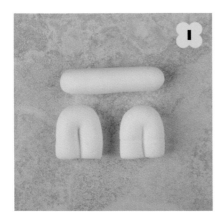

1 **Legs (make 2)** With the white paste, roll a sausage shape and fold it over to make two legs. Trim the bottom of the legs with the knife.

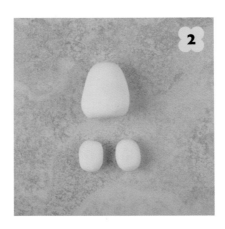

2 **Body and shoes** Make a rounded triangle shape for the body. Roll 2 ovals for the shoes and press to flatten slightly.

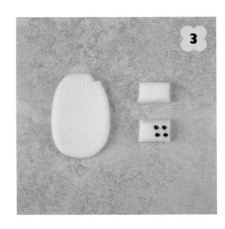

3 **Belly plate** Roll out some white paste. Cut a little rectangle from it and add 4 little dots with the black edible-ink pen.

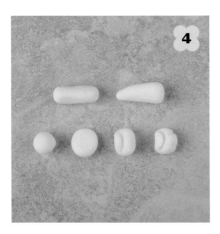

4 **Arms and hands (make 2)** Roll a teardrop shape for the arm. Start with a ball for the hand, flatten slightly and then fold over to make a fist.

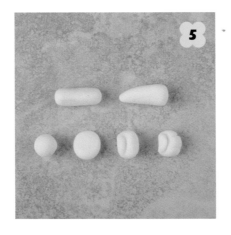

5 **Backpack** Roll some white modelling paste about ¼in (6mm) thick, cut a rectangle and add horizontal lines. Roll a small sausage shape and trim the edges to make a breathing pipe.

6 **Helmet** Roll a white ball for the helmet and cut out a small black circle from black modelling paste for the front of the helmet.

7 **Assemble** Attach the feet to the legs, then the body with the belly plate. Add the arms and hands, then the helmet. Finally, add the backpack and breathing pipe.

8 **Finish off** Completely cover your cupcake with marbled grey, black and white sugarpaste (see page 142). Use a large and small ball tool to make craters. Add your astronaut.

Tip

If you're having a party for a budding astronaut, why not make some Moon rocket cakes too (see page 102)? You could also leave some cakes plain and just decorate them with cut-out stars.

This snappy little creature with a broad grin is cleverly assembled so he lounges on a water-effect cupcake. The crocodile will certainly liven up the table at any party.

Cunning crocodile

You will need:

Dark green modelling paste

Leaf- and flower-shaping tool

White sugarpaste

Sugar glue

Craft knife

White modelling paste

2 x ⅛in (4mm) black sugar balls

Small ball tool

Blue sugarpaste

Cupcake (see page 138)

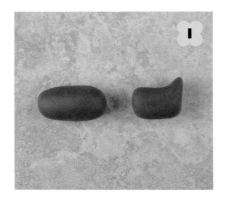

1 Head Roll a fat sausage shape with dark green modelling paste. Press the back of it up and flatten it. Flatten the front a little for the nostrils.

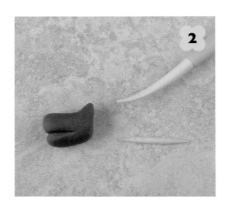

2 Mouth Use a leaf- and flower-shaping tool to indent a mouth on the head. Roll a long, thin white piece of white sugarpaste, thinner at both ends.

3 Teeth Put a little sugar glue on the indented mouth and glue the white low into the indent for the teeth. Use the craft knife to etch 'v' shapes in the white paste to make teeth.

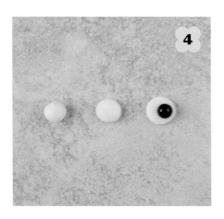

4 Eyes (make 2) Roll a white ball from modelling paste and flatten it a little. Use a black sugar ball for the eyeball.

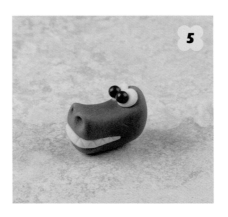

5 Face Add the eyes to the flatter part of the face and make nostrils with the small ball tool.

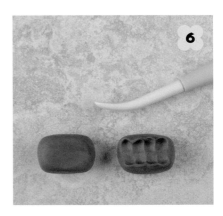

6 Body Using some dark green modelling paste, shape a round-edged rectangle for the body and use the leaf- and flower-shaping tool to make a row of grooves on the back.

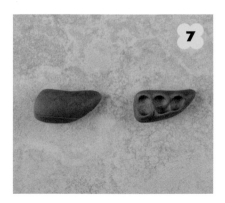

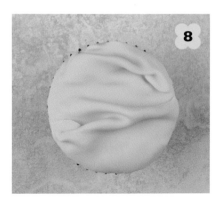

7 **Tail** Make a long triangle shape from dark green modelling paste and bend slightly for the end of the tail. Use the leaf- and flower-shaping tool to make grooves in the tail.

8 **Water** Cover the cupcake with blue sugarpaste to create a water-effect covered cupcake (see page 144).

9 **Finish off** Add the head, body and tail between the folds of 'water' on the cupcake.

This very pretty crown, wand and flowers cupcake will suit any little girl's princess-themed party table and would go well with the flower-girl cupcake on pages 14–17.

Princess crown

You will need:

Light pink modelling paste

Crown template (see page 152)

Sugar glue

4 x ⅛in (4mm) ivory sugar balls

Star cutter

Medium pink modelling paste

Medium 5-petal cutter and multi-veiner set

Medium daisy-centre stamp

Petunia cutter and veiner set

2 x ⅓in (8mm) white sugar pearls

White modelling paste

Primrose cutter

Dark pink sugarpaste

Cupcake (see page 138)

Vanilla buttercream (see page 140)

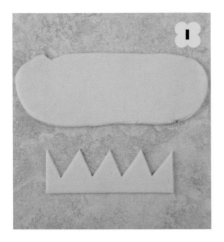

1 **Crown** Roll out some light pink modelling paste to about ⅛–⅙in (3–4mm) thick and use the template on page 152 to cut out a crown.

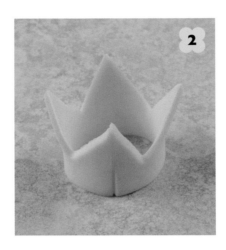

2 **Crown** Wrap the crown around and seal it at the back with a little sugar glue.

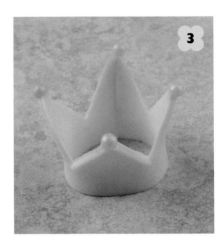

3 **Crown tips** Curve into a crown shape and add an ivory sugar ball to the tip of each crown peak with a little sugarpaste.

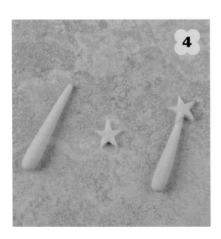

4 **Wand** Roll a long teardrop shape. Cut out a star and attach it to the pointed end of the wand.

5 **Imprinted flower** From medium pink modelling paste, cut out a medium 5-petal flower and use the multi-veiner to add detail.

6 **Flower centre** Use a daisy-centre stamp to make a white centre to finish off the flower.

7 **Petunia** Use the petunia cutter and veiner to cut out a light pink flower. Finish off with a white sugar pearl.

8 **Primrose** Cut out a white flower with the primrose cutter and finish off with a white sugar pearl.

9 **Finish off** Cover your cupcake with sugarpaste (see page 142) and put a swirl of buttercream on top. Add all the decorations to finish.

This cute little elephant, who's having fun cooling herself off in the water with perfectly crafted little water droplets, will be perfect for your wild little party!

Ellie the elephant

You will need:

Grey modelling paste

Craft knife

Small ball tool

Heart cutter

2 x ⅙in (4mm) black sugar balls

Black edible-ink pen

Sugar glue

Light blue modelling paste

Light blue sugarpaste

Cupcake (see page 138) covered with dark green sugarpaste (see page 142)

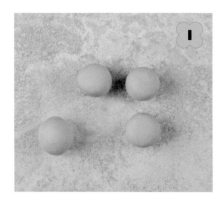

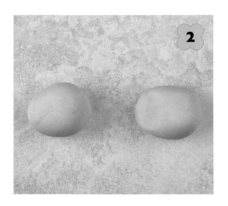

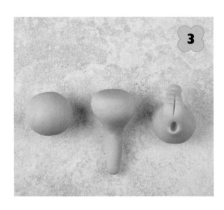

1 Legs Roll 4 balls from grey modelling paste and press them flat.

2 Body Roll a ball and shape into an oval. Use your thumb to press down the front of the body for the head to sit on.

3 Head Roll a ball and shape a trunk out of the front of the face. Bend the trunk up and back over the face. Use the craft knife to add some lines under the trunk. Use a small ball tool to make a mouth.

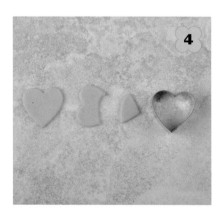

4 Ears (make 2) Use a heart cutter to cut a heart shape and then cut into the heart with the side of the heart cutter.

5 Face Add the black sugar balls for eyes. Draw on eyebrows with edible-ink pen. Attach the ears to the side of the head with sugar glue.

6 Tail Roll a teardrop shape, press the larger end flat and cut into it to make the tail hair.

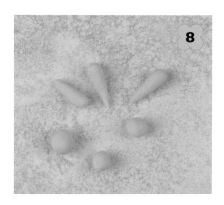

7 **Assemble** Add the body to the legs. Use sugar glue to attach the head to the body, and add the tail.

8 **Water droplets** With blue modelling paste, roll 3 teardrop shapes and 3 little balls for water coming out of the trunk and droplets on the elephant's back.

9 **Finish off** Half cover the iced cupcake with blue icing to give a water effect (see page 144). Add the elephant, facing the 'water'. Add droplets to the trunk and the elephant's back.

This one is sure to draw admiration from the grown-ups.
A cocktail in a coconut shell and bright flowers make the Hawaiian luau
the perfect cupcake for any beach-themed or tropical summer party.

Hawaiian luau

You will need:

Dark brown modelling paste

Large ball tool

Shell tool

Dark pink modelling paste

Bright orange modelling paste (mix melon and tangerine paste colour)

Craft knife

Heart cutter

Medium 5-petal cutter

Small primrose cutter

Bright green modelling paste (mix melon and party green paste colour)

Sugar glue

⅓in (8mm) sugar pearls – blue, white and green

Petunia cutter and veiner set

Large blossom cutter and veiner set

Yellow modelling paste

Large blossom plunger cutter

Medium blossom plunger cutter

Blue modelling paste

3 x ⅙in (4mm) pink sugar balls

Clear piping gel

Blue sugarpaste

Cupcake (see page 138)

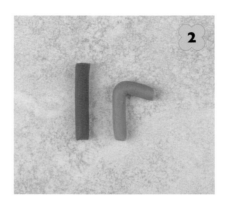

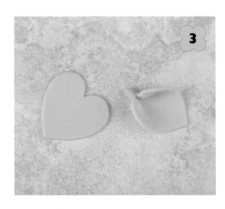

1 Coconut cup With dark brown modelling paste, roll a ball. Use the ball tool to make an indent in the ball. With the shell tool, 'scratch' the sides of the cup to give it a hairy effect.

2 Straws Roll a pink and an orange sausage shape and trim the ends with the craft knife. Bend the orange straw over for effect.

3 Leaf With the heart cutter, cut out a heart and fold the rounded ends to create a leaf (see page 151).

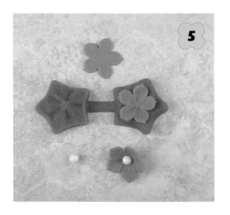

4 Double flower Cut a dark pink medium 5-petal flower. Cut out a small bright green primrose flower. Stick the green primrose on to the pink flower with sugar glue and finish off with a blue sugar pearl.

5 Petunia Use the petunia cutter and veiner set to create an orange flower and finish off with a white sugar pearl.

6 Large blossom Use your large blossom cutter and veiner set to create a yellow flower and finish off with a green sugar pearl.

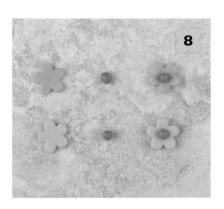

7 **Blossom** Use a large blossom plunger cutter to cut a pink flower and finish off with a blue sugar pearl.

8 **Medium blossoms** Use the medium blossom plunger cutter to cut out 1 orange and 1 blue flower. Finish them off with pink sugar balls.

9 **Cocktail** Add a little clear piping gel to the coconut cup and add the straws and the orange flower.

10 **Finish off** Cover the cupcake with blue sugarpaste (see page 142). Add the coconut to the middle of your cupcake and then add the flowers around it.

Having a winter-themed party? This delightful and very happy little penguin with her very own ice pool is bound to prove popular with all the children at the party table.

Pretty penguin

You will need:

Black modelling paste

Yellow modelling paste

White modelling paste

Heart cutter

Craft knife

Circle cutter

Medium blossom plunger cutter

Sugar glue

2 x ⅙in (4mm) black sugar balls

Cupcake (see page 138)

Buttercream

White sugarpaste

Large round cutter 3⅛in (78mm)

White icing

Piping gel

Blue paste colour

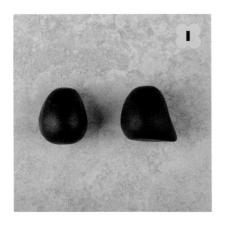

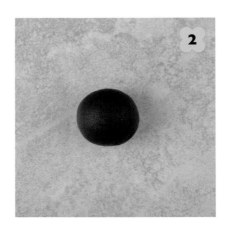

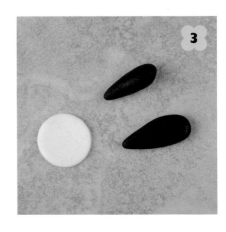

1 Body Make an oval shape from black modelling paste. Pinch it slightly at the back to make the tail.

2 Head Roll a ball for the head.

3 Belly and wings Cut out a white circle for the belly. Roll a black teardrop shape and flatten it to make a wing (make 2).

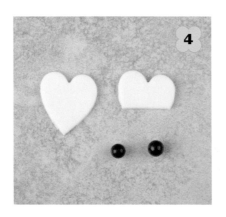

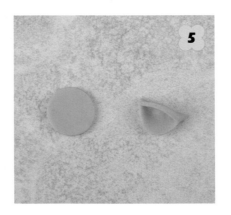

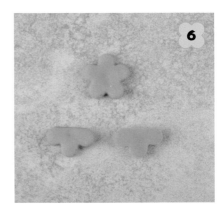

4 Face Cut out a white heart with the heart cutter and use the craft knife to trim off the pointed part of the heart.

5 Beak Cut a small circle with yellow modelling paste using the circle cutter. Bend it in half and pinch it at the sides so that the middle is left open and you have an smiley beak.

6 Feet Using the medium blossom plunger cutter, cut 1 flower about ⅛in (3mm) thick and cut it in half to make 2 feet.

7 **Assemble** Start by adding the wings to the belly with sugar glue. Put the head on the body. Add the face and beak. Use the black sugar balls for the eyes. Finally, add the feet.

8 **Cupcake detail** Ice the top of the cupcake with some buttercream. Use some white sugarpaste to roll a sausage shape and shape it into an 'o' on the cupcake.

9 **Cover cupcake** Use the large round cutter to cut a disk of icing to cover the cupcake, smoothing over the 'o' and creating a well (see page 142).

10 **Finish off** Colour some piping gel with a little blue paste colour to fill the well. Use sugar glue to stick the penguin on the side of her ice pool.

This adorable puppy-face cupcake would suit any animal or pet-themed party. Work on one cupcake at a time so that the sugarpaste stays soft and will be easy to smooth on.

Playful puppy

You will need:

Buttercream (see page 140)

Cupcake (see page 138)

White sugarpaste

Shell tool

Golden brown sugarpaste (mix a little dark brown with autumn leaf paste colour)

Round cookie cutter

Craft knife

Leaf- and flower-shaping tool

White modelling paste

Dark brown modelling paste

Sugar glue

Black modelling paste

2 very small circle cutters

2 x white nonpareils

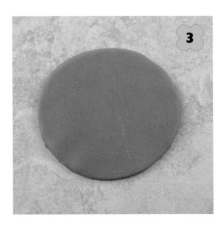

1 Snout Add buttercream to the top of the cupcake. Shape a snout out of it on the bottom half.

2 Cover cupcake Cover the cupcake with white sugarpaste and use the shell tool to scratch into the icing to give the impression of fur.

3 Disk Using the round cookie cutter, cut out a disk of golden brown sugarpaste.

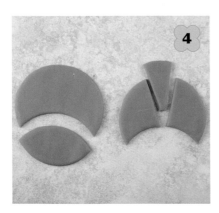

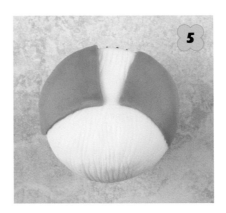

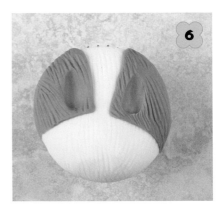

4 Patches Cut into the bottom of the disk with the round cutter to form a crescent-moon shape. Then cut a flat 'v' into the middle of the crescent with the craft knife.

5 Patches Add the patches to the sides of the face above the snout and smooth down the sides of the cupcake for a good finish.

6 Effects and eye sockets Use the shell tool to scratch into the brown sugarpaste to create a fur effect. Make two little teardrop-shaped eye sockets using the leaf- and flower-shaping tool, larger at the bottom than the top.

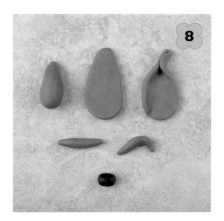

7 Eyes Roll two teardrop shapes from white modelling paste and press them flat. With the larger circle cutter, cut out 2 circles from dark brown modelling paste. Stick them at the thinner end of the white shapes with sugar glue. Cut 2 circles from black modelling paste with the smaller circle cutter, and stick them on to the brown circles, leaving a rim of brown visible as in the photo. Trim the sides and add a white nonpareil to each eye.

8 Ears and eyebrows (make 2) and nose Roll a teardrop shape from golden brown modelling paste and press the narrower side in on itself. Roll a small sausage shape and shape it into an eyebrow. Roll a black oval for the nose.

9 Finish off Add the nose, eyes, eyebrows and ears. Use the shell tool to scratch on the eyebrows and at the top of the ears to fit with the fur effect on the rest of the face.

Having a New Year, festive or milestone birthday party?
These charming little champagne-themed cupcakes look very
impressive and will brighten up any grown-up celebration.

Fizz and fun

You will need:

Dark green modelling paste

Large ball tool

White modelling paste

Craft knife

Black edible-ink pen

Sugar glue

Small paintbrush

Light blue modelling paste

Yellow modelling paste

Red modelling paste

Bright green modelling paste

Piping gel

Autumn leaf paste colour

White nonpareils

White sugarpaste

Cupcake (see page 138)

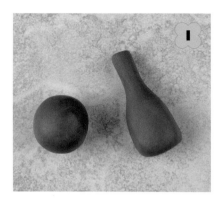

1 Bottle Roll a ball and shape into a bottle. Trim the top of the bottle neck and use a large ball tool to indent the bottom of the bottle.

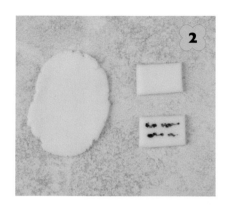

2 Label Roll out some white modelling paste and cut a little label for the bottle. Use an edible-ink pen to make little squiggles to represent writing on the label.

3 Bottle Using sugar glue, add the label to the front of the bottle.

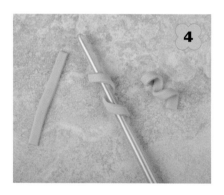

4 Streamers Roll out a little blue modelling paste and cut a thin strip. Wrap the strip around the end of a paintbrush then gently pull it off the end to make a streamer. Do the same with the yellow, red and green modelling paste.

5 Details Colour some piping gel with autumn leaf paste colour. Pour out some white nonpareils.

6 Cover cupcake Cover the cupcake with white sugarpaste (see page 142). Add the bottle to your cupcake. Add the piping gel for spilt champagne and sprinkle some white nonpareils over the top for bubbles.

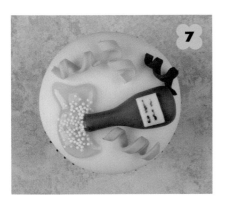

7 Finish off Finish off the cupcake by adding the streamers.

Tip

If you are making lots of cupcakes, save a bit of time by decorating some of them just with colourful streamers.

This wise little owl can be used for parties for grown-ups and kids. If you need something cute, bright and colourful for a party table, this little cupcake will fit the bill.

Wise owl

You will need:

Dark pink modelling paste

Dark brown modelling paste

Medium pink modelling paste

Medium daisy plunger cutter

Craft knife

Blue modelling paste

2 smallest-sized circle cutters

⅛in (4mm) sugar balls – 2 pink, 3 white and 2 black

Yellow modelling paste

Cone tool

Sugar glue

Bright green modelling paste

(mix a little melon with party green paste colour)

Bright orange modelling paste

(mix a little melon with tangerine paste colour)

Small heart cutter

Medium blossom plunger cutter

Dark green sugarpaste

Cupcake (see page 138)

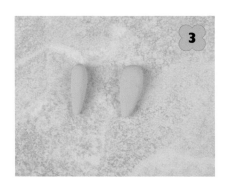

1 Body Roll a ball from dark pink modelling paste and shape pointed ears at the top of the body.

2 Belly feathers Cut 2 medium daisies with the daisy cutter from medium pink modelling paste. Use the craft knife to cut up the daisies as 4 petals, 3 petals and 2 petals. Build the 3 groups on top of each other, from 4 petals to 2 petals, to fit on the belly.

3 Wings (make 2) Roll a blue teardrop shape and press it flat.

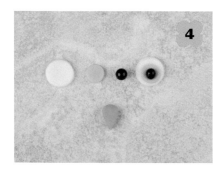

4 Eyes and beak Cut out 2 small white circles and 2 very small bright green circles. Place the green circles on the white ones and add black sugar balls. Shape a little yellow beak from yellow modelling paste and use the cone tool to make nostrils.

5 Feet Roll some bright orange paste to about 1/8in (3mm) thick and cut out a medium daisy. Cut the daisy into 2 x 3 petals for the feet.

6 Assemble With sugar glue, stick on the belly feathers, wings, eyes and beak to the body. Finish off with the feet.

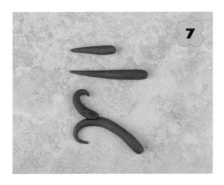

7 Branches Roll a small and a large teardrop shape from dark brown modelling paste and curl the thinner ends.

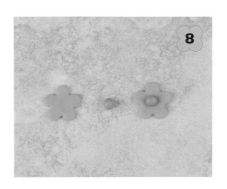

8 Flowers Make up 3 pink and 2 yellow flowers using the medium blossom plunger cutter and finish off with little white and pink sugar balls.

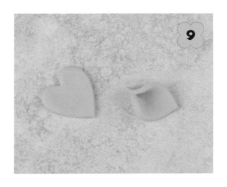

9 Leaves (make 3) Create a bright green leaf using the heart cutter (see page 151).

10 Finish off Cover the cupcake with dark green sugarpaste (see page 142). Add the branches to the cupcake. Place the owl sitting on the branches and add the flowers and leaves.

This cute little witch sitting on her broom would be perfect for a Halloween party. You could pair her up with the wizard character on pages 118–121.

Wilma witch

You will need:

Black modelling paste

Flesh pink modelling paste (mix chestnut and cream paste colour)

Craft knife

Scallop tool

Piece of uncooked spaghetti for support

2 x black nonpareils

Small ball tool

Medium circle cutter

Sugar glue

Bright green modelling paste (mix melon and party green paste colour)

Chestnut brown modelling paste

Dark brown modelling paste

Shell tool

A little vegetable fat

Sugarcraft gun with grass/hair disk

Bright green sugarpaste

Cupcake (see page 138)

Dark purple modelling paste

Large star plunger cutter

1 Body/dress Roll a ball from black modelling paste and shape it into a cone shape with a rounded top.

2 Support Push the piece of spaghetti into the body to add support.

3 Head Roll a ball from flesh pink modelling paste. Trim the top of the head with the craft knife. Make a smile with the scallop tool.

4 Face Add 2 black nonpareils for the eyes. Roll a little flesh pink paste nose and add it to the face.

5 Sleeves and hands (make 2 of each) Make a black teardrop shape for the sleeve. Use the small ball tool to make a hole in each sleeve. To make the hand, roll a flesh pink paste ball, press it flat and cut a small 'v' for the thumb. Shape a little wrist to fit into the sleeve.

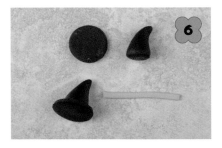

6 Hat Cut a black circle with the medium circle cutter. Roll a cone shape and bend the pointed end. Use sugar glue to stick the hat to the base. Cut a thin strip of bright green modelling paste for the hat trim and wrap it around the base of the hat.

7 **Broom and shoes** Roll a sausage shape in chestnut brown paste for the handle. Cut a small rectangle of dark brown paste and roll a cone shape in the same colour, bending the pointed end slightly. Use a shell tool to add detail for bristles. Make up the broom. Roll 2 chestnut brown ovals for the shoes.

8 **Assemble** Attach the head to the body.

9 **Hair** Add the witch's hair (see page 147).

10 **Assemble figure** Add the shoes. Make 2 buttons from bright green modelling paste by rolling a small ball and indenting it with the small ball tool. Add the sleeves, with the hands attached to the ends, and glue the hat to the top of the head.

11 **Finish off** Cover the cupcake with bright green sugarpaste (see page 142). Add the broom and the witch to the top of the cupcake. Cut out some large dark purple stars with the large star plunger cutter and glue onto the cupcake for extra detail.

3-2-1 blast off! This delightful little rocket racing through the cosmos would be perfect for a space-themed party. You could make the astronaut cupcake on pages 62–65 to go with it.

Moon rocket

You will need:

White modelling paste

Craft knife

Sugar glue

Grey modelling paste

Cone tool

Red modelling paste

Yellow modelling paste

Large star plunger cutter

Light blue modelling paste

Plain cupcake

Black sugarpaste

Cupcake (see page 138)

A selection of metallic sugar balls

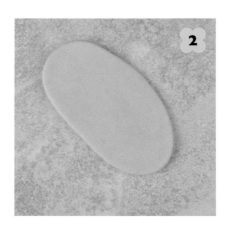

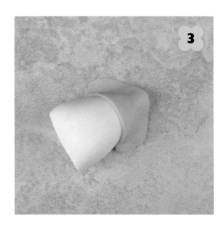

1 **Rocket** Using white modelling paste, make a large triangular shape for the rocket body and trim the bottom of it with a craft knife.

2 **Rocket front** Roll out grey paste to form an oval about ½₀in (1mm) thick.

3 **Front** Add a little glue to the pointed end of the rocket. Drape the grey paste over the glue, then shape it over the front of the rocket, smoothing the edges.

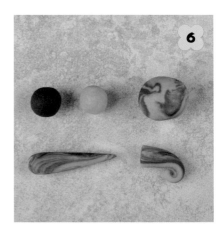

4 **Front** Trim the edges of the front to finish it off. Use the pointed tip of the cone tool to make little rivets on the edges of the grey top of the rocket.

5 **Fins (make 3)** Roll some white paste into teardrop shapes. Press them flat and bend them slightly to the side.

6 **Flames (make 3)** Mix red and yellow paste to create a marble effect. Roll a long teardrop shape and curl in the pointed end. Trim off the fatter end.

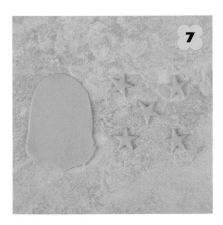

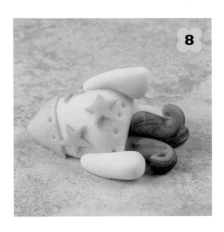

7 **Stars** With the star plunger cutter, cut out 5 blue stars to make the rocket detail.

8 **Assemble** Add some sugar glue to the back of the rocket and glue the fire, fins and stars to the rocket.

9 **Finish off** Cover the cupcake with black sugarpaste (see page 142). Add the rocket to your cupcake and add some metallic balls as planets.

Tip

If you're decorating lots of cakes why not add just stars and metallic balls to some of them to save time?

Off to a baby shower? Well, you need some special little cupcakes for the mum-to-be. These little booties, rattles and flowers will bring a smile to any expectant mum's face.

Baby shower

You will need:

Pale yellow modelling paste

Pale purple modelling paste

Sugar glue

Ball tool

Small round piping tip

White modelling paste

Light green modelling paste

Medium blossom plunger cutter

2 x ⅓in (8mm) white sugar balls

Heart cutter

Petunia cutter and veiner set

2 x ⅓in (8mm) white sugar pearls

Large blossom plunger cutter

Pale yellow sugarpaste

Cupcake (see page 138)

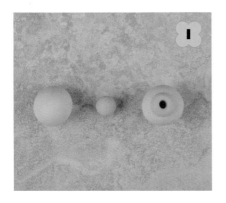

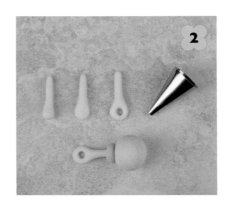

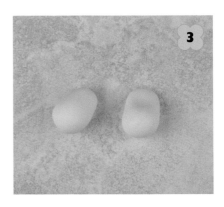

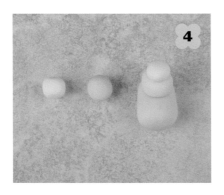

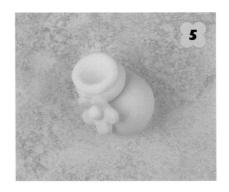

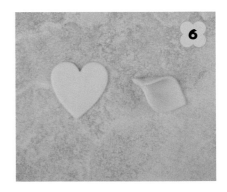

1 **Rattle** Roll a yellow ball and a smaller purple ball. Attach the two together with a little sugar glue and use a ball tool to make a hole through the purple piece.

2 **Handle** Roll a teardrop shape. Flatten the larger side slightly. Use the small round piping tip to cut out a little hole in the flattened end. Use some sugar glue on the end to push the handle into the rattle.

3 **Booties (make 2)** Roll a fat oval shape, one half narrower than the other. Press the narrower side down with your thumb to create the back of the bootie.

4 **Socks (make 2)** Roll a small white ball and a larger green ball. Attach the green one on top of the back of the bootie and then the white ball on top of that. Use a ball tool to press them into each other.

5 **Booties (make 2)** Use a medium blossom plunger cutter to add a little flower to each bootie and finish with a white sugar ball.

6 **Leaf** Cut out a heart shape with the heart cutter and fold the round parts in on each other to make a leaf (see page 151).

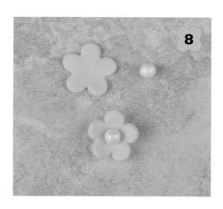

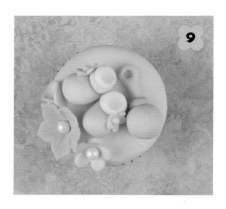

7 **Petunia** Use the petunia cutter and veiner set to create a purple flower. Finish off with a white sugar pearl.

8 **Blossom** Use a large blossom plunger cutter to cut out a yellow flower, and finish it off with a white sugar pearl in the centre.

9 **Finish off** Cover the cupcake with pale yellow sugarpaste. Add the booties, rattle, leaf and flowers to your cupcake to complete your project.

Tip

This would make a lovely gift for a new mother. Once the baby has been born you can of course choose your colours depending on whether it's a boy or a girl.

You will thoroughly enjoy creating this beautiful mermaid,
with her gorgeous tail, sweet little bikini and beautiful long hair.
She's sure to make waves at any party.

Merry mermaid

You will need:

Cupcake (see page 138)

Buttercream

Sugarpaste

Sugar glue

Large round cutter 3¹⁄₁₆in (78mm)

Marbled sugarpaste (mix white, black and grey paste together)

Dark pink modelling paste

Sugar glue

Scallop tool

Craft knife

Flesh pink modelling paste
   (mix a little chestnut with cream paste colour)

Piece of uncooked spaghetti

2 x black nonpareils

Cone tool

Dark brown modelling paste

A little vegetable fat

Sugarcraft gun with grass/hair disk

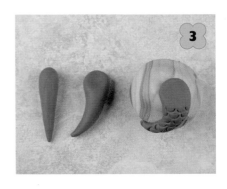

1 **Rock** Add buttercream to your cupcake. Use some sugarpaste to build up a rock shape on your cupcake.

2 **Covering** Using the large round cutter, cut out a disk from your marbled sugarpaste. Use it to cover the top of the cake (see page 142).

3 **Tail** Roll a big teardrop shape with dark pink modelling paste, press the top flat and curl the tail end slightly. Glue on to the rock with sugar glue and use the scallop tool to make the scales on the tail.

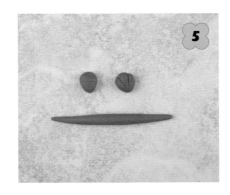

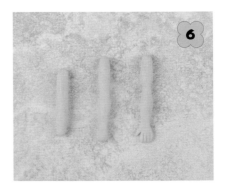

4 **Body** Using flesh pink modelling paste, shape the body with a neck, stick onto the tail and add a piece of spaghetti for support. Add the tail tip.

5 **Bikini cup (make 2) and waistband** Using dark pink modelling paste, roll a rounded triangular shape and flatten it a little. Use a craft knife to make the shell detail. Roll out a long sausage shape, thinner at the ends, for the waistband.

6 **Arms and hands (make 2)** Using flesh pink modelling paste, roll out a sausage shape. Indent for the elbow and hand, press the hand flat and cut a small 'v' for the thumb. Use a craft knife to mark the other fingers (see page 146).

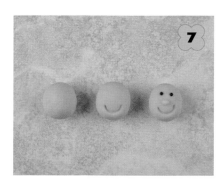

7 **Face** Make a ball shape. Make a smile with a scallop tool and form a little ball for the nose. Add black two nonpareils for the eyes.

8 **Assemble** Add the mermaid's bikini. Give her a little belly button using a cone tool, and then add the waistband. Attach the arms and head with sugar glue.

9 **Hair** Add some vegetable fat to the dark brown modelling paste and add the mermaid's hair (see page 147).

Tip
A collection of mermaids with different coloured hair and bikinis will look stunning on a party table.

A woodland-themed party table wouldn't be complete without this delightful little critter hugging his precious acorn in a sweet forest scene with different-coloured flowers.

Sweet squirrel

You will need:

Dark brown modelling paste

Chestnut brown modelling paste

Craft knife

Small ball tool

⅛in (4mm) sugar balls – 2 black, 2 pink and 1 white

Black modelling paste

Sugar glue

Hydrangea cutter and veiner set

Blue modelling paste

Medium blossom plunger cutter

Yellow modelling paste

Pink modelling paste

Dark green sugarpaste

Cupcake (see page 138)

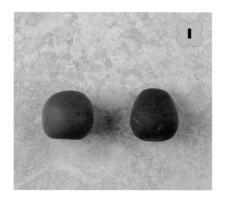

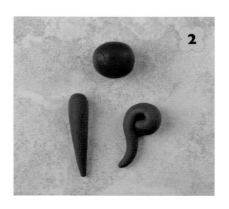

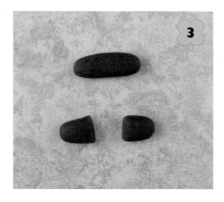

1 **Body** Roll a ball from dark brown modelling paste and shape into a body with a smaller rounded top.

2 **Head and tail** Roll a small ball for the head. Roll a long teardrop shape from chestnut brown modelling paste for the tail and curl the tail in on itself at the fatter end.

3 **Hands and feet (make 2)** Roll a dark brown sausage shape and press it flat. Cut it in half with a craft knife. The hands and feet are the same.

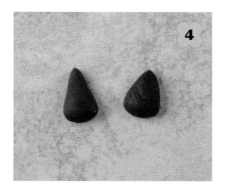

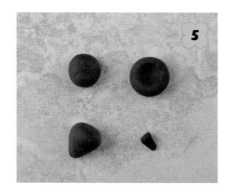

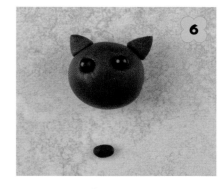

4 **Ears (make 2)** Roll a small dark brown cone and flatten it.

5 **Acorn** Roll a dark brown ball. Using the ball tool, make an indent in the ball to make the acorn cup. For the acorn, roll a little fat cone shape in chestnut brown, with a pointed bottom. Roll a little stem with dark brown modelling paste.

6 **Face** Add the ears and 2 black sugar balls for eyes. Make a little oval black nose and attach it with sugar glue.

7 Assemble Add the feet, head and tail to the body.

8 Hands and acorn Use sugar glue to stick the hands to each side of the acorn and then glue to the body.

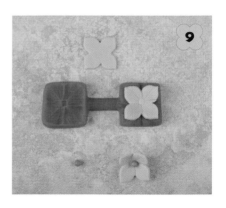

9 Hydrangea Use the hydrangea cutter and veiner to make a blue flower. Finish it off with a pink sugar ball.

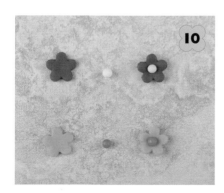

10 Little blossoms Cut a pink and a yellow flower with the medium blossom plunger cutter and finish with a white and a pink sugar ball.

11 Finish off Cover the cupcake with dark green sugarpaste (see page 142). Complete the cupcake by adding the squirrel and flowers.

This magical wizard with his deep purple cloak and long white beard would be a suitable accompaniment to any magic-themed party and would be great for Halloween.

Wily wizard

You will need:

Dark purple modelling paste

Flesh pink modelling paste (mix a little chestnut with cream paste colour)

Craft knife

Ball tool

Black modelling paste

Scallop tool

White icing

2 x black nonpareils

White modelling paste

A little vegetable fat

Sugarcraft gun with hair/grass disk

Medium and large star plunger cutter

Bright green modelling paste (mix a little melon with party green paste colour)

Bright green sugarpaste

Cupcake (see page 138)

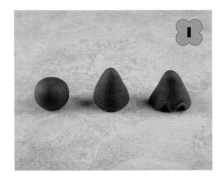

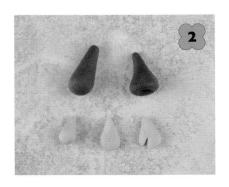

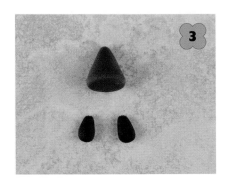

1 **Cloak** Roll a ball with dark purple modelling paste and shape into a cone. Press around the bottom of the cloak to flatten it a little.

2 **Sleeves and hands** Roll some teardrop-shaped sleeves from dark purple modelling paste and flatten at the ends. Use the ball tool to make holes in the end of the sleeves. Roll teardrop shapes from flesh pink modelling paste for the hands. Press them flat and cut a 'V' for the thumb with the craft knife.

3 **Shoes and hat** Roll 2 dark black oval shapes and flatten them a little for the shoes. Roll out a small cone shape for the hat.

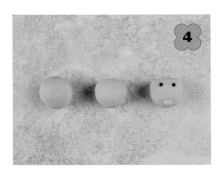

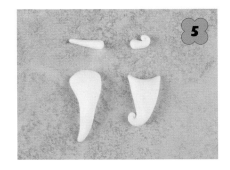

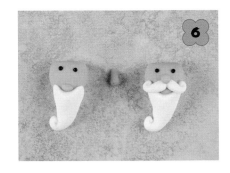

4 **Face** Roll a ball of flesh pink paste and trim off the top. Use the scallop tool to make a smile. Add a small piece of white icing for the lip and 2 small black nonpareils for eyes.

5 **Beard** Roll 2 very small teardrop shapes from white modelling paste for the moustache. Roll in the pointed ends to make a curl. Roll a bigger teardrop shape for the beard. Roll up the bottom and shape the top sides to fit the face.

6 **Assemble face** Attach the beard just under the lip and roll a little teardrop shape from flesh pink paste for the nose. Add the moustache above the lip and then the nose in the middle of the moustache.

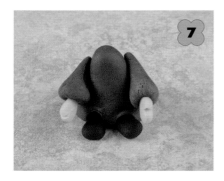

7 **Assemble body** Add the shoes to the front of the cloak and add the sleeves and hands.

8 Attach the head to the body.

9 **Hair** Add white hair to the sides of his head (see page 147). Leave the top of the head bald for the hat to sit on.

10 **Stars** Cut out 7 large purple stars for the cupcake and 4 small bright green stars for the hat.

11 Cover the cupcake with bright green sugarpaste (see page 142). Add the wizard and stars to the cupcake.

Need a special cupcake for a special occasion? This elegant
flower-embellished cake can be made up for any event,
even if it's just to say 'thank you' or 'get well'.

Say it with flowers

You will need:

Dark green modelling paste

Red flower/petal paste

Medium 5-petal cutter

Foam mat

Ball tool

Sugar glue

Drying foam

Large daisy-centre stamp

White modelling paste

Large blossom cutter and veiner set

Black modelling paste

1 x ⅓in (8mm) red sugar pearl

White sugarpaste

Cupcake (see page 138)

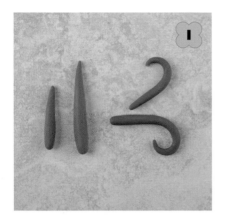

1 **Stems** Roll out 2 teardrop-shaped stems from dark green modelling paste, with one longer than the other. Curl the pointed side in on itself.

2 **Flowers** Roll out red flower paste thinner than ½₀in (1mm) and cut out 3 medium 5-petal flowers with the 5-petal cutter.

3 **Flaring** On the foam mat, run the ball tool around the edges of the petal to flare it. Do this on all 3 flowers.

4 **Assemble** Overlap the three flowers so you can see all the petals. Stick the flowers together using a little sugar glue in the middle of them.

5 **Drying** Set the flower into the drying foam and leave to dry.

6 **Centre** Use a large daisy-centre stamp to make a white centre for the flower.

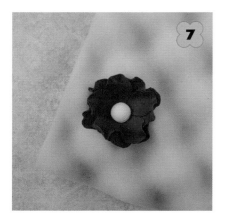

7 **Assemble** Add the centre to the flower with a little sugar glue.

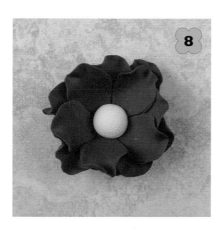

8 **Dried flower** Wait until your flower is properly dried out before removing it from the foam. If possible, leave it overnight.

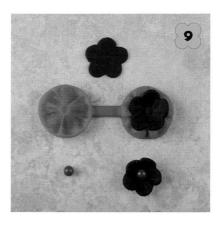

9 **Blossom** Use the large blossom cutter and veiner to create a black flower and finish off with a red sugar pearl at the centre.

10 **Finish off** Cover the cupcake in white sugarpaste (see page 142). Add the green curled stems to the cupcake and then the red and black flowers.

No need for winter to be bleak! This bright and cheerful snowman, wrapped up in his jaunty hat and scarf, on a snowy cupcake will add lots of cheer and colour to a winter-themed party table.

Sid the snowman

You will need:

White modelling paste
Craft knife
Small ball tool
2 x ⅙in (4mm) black sugar balls
Orange modelling paste
Scallop tool
Red modelling paste

Yellow modelling paste
Design wheel with stitching wheel tool
Dark brown modelling paste
Blue modelling paste
White sugarpaste
Cupcake (see page 138)

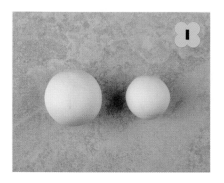

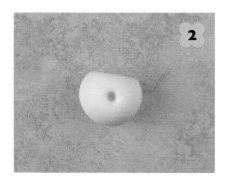

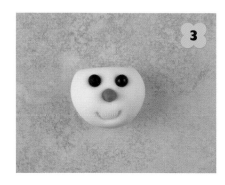

1 **Body and head** Roll 2 balls from white modelling paste, 1 large for the belly and 1 smaller for the head.

2 **Head** Trim the top of the head with a craft knife. Using the small ball tool, make a little hole in the middle of the face for the nose.

3 **Face** Add 2 black sugar balls for eyes. Roll a carrot-shaped nose in orange modelling paste. Use sugar glue to stick the nose into the hole. Use the scallop tool to make a smile on the face.

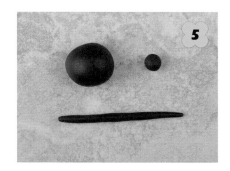

4 **Body** Stick the head to the body with sugar glue and make 2 holes for the arms with the small ball tool.

5 **Hat** Make the hat by rolling a red ball and pressing it flat underneath to allow it to fit on the head. Make a small ball for the bauble and roll a long sausage shape for the trim.

6 **Assembling the hat** Use sugar glue to stick the larger ball on to the snowman's head. Wrap the trim around the hat. Use a craft knife to add vertical lines around the trim and hat. Glue the bauble to the top of the hat.

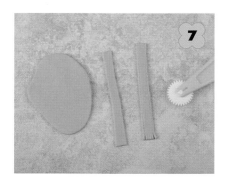

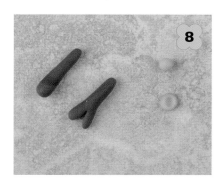

7 **Scarf** Roll out some yellow paste and cut a strip for the scarf. Use the stitching tool to add detail on the edges and the craft knife to cut into the ends of the scarf to make tassels.

8 **Arms and buttons (make 2 of each)** Roll a teardrop shape in brown modelling paste and slightly flatten the fatter side. Cut a little way down the middle of the fatter side to create a hand, and leave to dry a little. Roll a small blue ball and indent it with the ball tool to make a button.

9 **Assemble** Wrap the scarf around the snowman's neck, add his buttons and put sugar glue in the armholes to stick on the arms.

10 **Finish off** Cover the cupcake in white sugarpaste (see page 142). Add the snowman to the cupcake. Roll a few white balls to make snowballs.

Techniques

How to get your cupcakes ready to party

Equipment for decorating

PME leaf- and flower-shaping tool

PME scallop and comb tool

PME shell and blade tool

PME ball tool

PME bulbous cone tool

PME stitching wheel tool

Plastic spatula

Lace embossing texture mat

Rolling pin

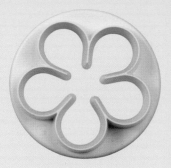

5-petal flower cutter

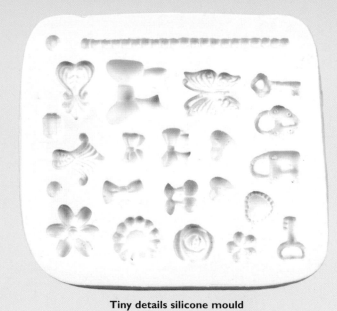

Tiny details silicone mould

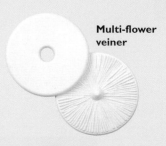

Multi-flower veiner

Set of round and scalloped cookie cutters

Sugarcraft gun

Large star nozzle

Craft knife

Fine paintbrush for painting

Paintbrush for glue

Foam drying sheet (egg-box foam)

Wilton leaf cutter

Circle cutter set

Heart cutter set

**PME daisy,
blossom and star
plunger cutters**

**JEM daisy-
centre
stamps**

Hydrangea cutter and veiner set

Small blossom cutter and veiner set

Flower foam mat

Petunia cutter and veiner set

Large blossom cutter and veiner set

Clear stamps

Paint palette

Primrose cutters

Small circle cookie cutter

Ingredients for decorating

Coloured sugarpaste and coloured modelling paste

Black edible-ink pen

Natural piping jelly

Rejuvenator fluid

Buttercream

Nonpareils

White sugarpaste (flower or petal paste)

⅛in (4mm) sugar balls

⅓in (8mm) sugar pearls

Vegetable fat, such as Trex

Uncooked spaghetti

Colours used in the book

Basic colours

Tangerine

Grape/Violet

Caramel

Foliage green extra

Dark brown

Red extra

Ice blue

Rose pink

Black extra

Party green

Cream

Melon

Egg yellow

Chestnut brown

Mixed colours

Bright green: party green mixed with melon

Grey: white mixed with a little black

Bright orange: tangerine mixed with melon

Puppy patches: caramel with a little chestnut brown

Flesh pink: cream mixed with a touch of chestnut brown

Here is a selection of colours I have used in this book, including the shades that can be achieved by combining different colours. I mainly use Sugarflair colourings, but there are many other excellent products available.

Cupcake recipes

Vanilla cupcakes

Makes 12 cupcakes

You will need
6oz (175g) caster sugar
6oz (175g) plain flour
6oz (175g) butter
3 eggs
1 teaspoon vanilla essence
1 teaspoon baking powder
12 cupcake cases
Muffin tray

Tip
Always bake on the low temperatures indicated to produce rounded cupcakes that do not peak in the middle. These cupcakes will be perfect to cover with sugarpaste.

1 Preheat your oven to 260°F (130°C) for a fan oven, 280°F (140°C) for an electric oven, or gas mark 2.

2 Put the sugar in a bowl.

3 Sift the flour over the sugar.

4 Add the rest of the ingredients and mix them together in an electric mixer or with an electric hand mixer until light and creamy.

5 Put the cupcake cases in the muffin tray and fill them just over half full.

6 Bake for 25–30 minutes or until golden brown.

Chocolate cupcakes

Makes 18 cupcakes

You will need

8oz (250g) caster sugar
4oz (140g) butter
2 eggs
2 teaspoons vanilla essence
1oz (55g) self-raising flour
5oz (165g) plain flour
¾ teaspoon bicarbonate of soda
2oz (60g) cocoa powder
7fl oz (210ml) milk
18 cupcake cases
Muffin tray

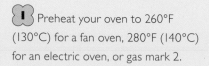 Preheat your oven to 260°F (130°C) for a fan oven, 280°F (140°C) for an electric oven, or gas mark 2.

2 Beat the sugar and butter in an electric mixer or with an electric hand mixer until light and fluffy.

3 Add the eggs and vanilla essence to the mixer and beat until well mixed.

4 Sift together the flours, bicarbonate of soda and cocoa powder.

5 Add the sifted ingredients and milk to the butter mixture and mix again until a creamy light brown colour.

6 In the muffin tray, fill the cupcake cases about ¾ full and bake for 25–30 minutes until they are cooked through. Check by inserting a cocktail stick or knife into the middle of a cake; if it comes out clean, the cakes are done.

Recipes for decoration

Modelling paste

You will need

1 teaspoon gum tragacanth powder or Tylo powder (CMC)
250g white sugarpaste or pre-coloured sugarpaste of your choice

1 Add the gum tragacanth to the sugarpaste.

2 Knead the sugarpaste until all the gum tragacanth powder is well mixed in

3 You can use the paste immediately if you need to, but it is better to leave it overnight in a sealed plastic bag to 'settle' and firm up a little.

Sugar glue

You will need

Sugarpaste
Boiling water
Plastic tub with a lid

1 Break up some sugarpaste into little pieces and place in the plastic tub.

2 Pour boiled water over the sugarpaste and leave it to cool a bit.

3 When it has cooled to room temperature, stir it with a teaspoon. You should have a slightly milky-coloured sugar glue.

4 Put the lid on the tub and use as needed. Sugar glue should be kept in the fridge and used within one month.

Buttercream

You will need

4oz (115g) unsalted butter or margarine
13oz (375g) icing sugar (confectioner's sugar)
2 tablespoons milk
2–4 tablespoons of unsweetened cocoa powder for chocolate buttercream

1 Beat the butter until it is light and fluffy.

2 If making chocolate buttercream, add the cocoa powder to the milk.

3 Gradually add the milk and icing sugar (on a slow speed if using an electric mixer).

4 Increase the speed of the mixer and continue to beat until the mixture becomes paler and is light enough in consistency to spread easily.

Sugarpaste

Sometimes referred to as fondant or roll-out icing, sugarpaste is readily available in sugarcraft shops and supermarkets. Sugarpaste can be bought in white or in a variety of ready-made colours. Using ready-coloured paste can save a lot of time, especially when using darker colours such as red, green or black.

You can also colour your own dark colours by using the following pastes by Sugarflair: Red Extra, Black Extra and Foliage Green Extra. They are highly concentrated colours and you only need a little to darken your icing. These colours also develop a bit more if left in a sealed plastic bag overnight.

Colouring sugarpaste and modelling paste

I colour all my sugarpaste and modelling paste myself. Only use paste colours to make up your colours. Using liquid colours will make the paste sticky and unusable.

You will need
White modelling paste
Colour for the paste
Cocktail stick

1 Use a cocktail stick to add the colour to the paste and knead it to achieve an even colour

2 For pale colours, only add a touch of colour to start with. If you need to, you can make it a little darker to build up the colour.

Preparing for decorations

Before you add characters and features to your cupcakes, you'll need to cover them with sugarpaste. You may also want to add piping or create a water or fabric texture on the top of the cupcake.

Sugarpaste dome-covered cupcake

You will need

Plain cupcake

Buttercream

Round cookie cutter, the size of the top of the cupcake

Sugarpaste

1 Start with a plain cupcake.

2 Add some buttercream to the middle of the cupcake with a spatula.

3 Cut out a disk with a round cookie cutter.

4 Add the sugarpaste disk to top of the cupcake.

5 Use the palm of your hand to smooth over the sugarpaste on the cupcake for a perfect finish.

Piping

You will need
Icing bag
Large open-star nozzle
Cupcake: plain or covered
  with sugarpaste

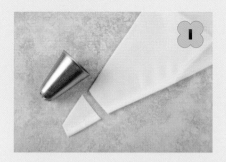

1 Cut the end of the icing bag to about ¾ of the height of your nozzle.

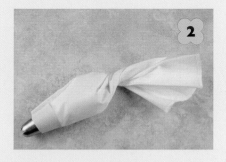

2 Push the nozzle to the end of the bag. Fill the bag with icing and twist the back of the bag to keep the icing in.

3 Start piping a swirl onto the cupcake. I always start from the inside and go outwards.

4 Follow the swirl around. Don't touch the icing with the nozzle while you're making the swirl, but let it fall naturally onto the cupcake.

5 Finish off the swirl in the middle at the top and gently press the nozzle down to finish it off.

Sugarpaste water or fabric effect

You will need

Plain cupcake

Blue sugarpaste

Sugar glue

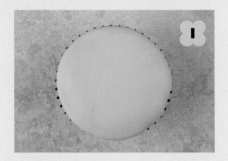

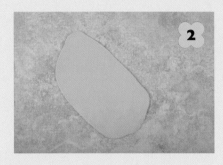

1 Cover the cupcake with blue sugarpaste.

2 Roll out some blue sugarpaste to about ½₀in (1mm) thick.

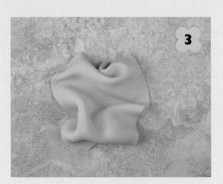

3 Gently 'gather' the sugarpaste together, being careful not to tear or damage it.

4 Add some sugar glue to the top of the cupcake and add the gathered sugarpaste. Bend, pinch and shape it into wave-like folds. Trim the sides neatly.

Making your decorations

There are some basic shapes you will need to learn to create the figures and details to decorate the top of your cupcakes. A couple of templates are provided for the Mini pirate on page 46 and the Princess crown on page 70.

Basic shapes

Sausage shape Roll a piece of icing or sugarpaste between your palms to stretch it out a bit and then roll it on your work mat to make it even.

Cone shape Roll a ball and then put your palms into a 'v' shape. Roll the ball in the 'v' to create a pointed top.

Teardrop shape Start off by rolling a sausage shape and then make a small 'v' in your hands to make a thinner, pointed side, leaving the other side rounded.

Legs

Roll a sausage shape. Indent it slightly at the knee and further down for the foot. Shape the foot and then use a craft knife to mark the toes.

Face

Roll a ball. Use a scallop tool to make the mouth. Roll a small ball for a nose and use black sugar balls for eyes or small black nonpareils for a small face.

Arms

Roll a sausage shape. Indent it slightly at the elbow and further down for the hand. Shape the hand and press it flat. Cut out a small 'v' for the thumb. Use a craft knife to mark the fingers.

Ears

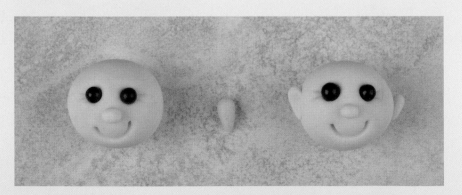

When you have finished the face, roll two small teardrop shapes for ears. Stick them to the side of the head with sugar glue, with the thinner end pointing towards the bottom of the head. Use a ball tool to smooth the ear onto the side of the head.

Hair and grass

You will need
Vegetable fat
Modelling paste
Sugarcraft gun
Grass/hair disk
Craft knife

To make hair, mix a little vegetable fat with some modelling paste. This gives you the perfect consistency for using a sugarcraft gun.

1 Add the modelling paste to the sugarcraft gun and use the grass/hair disk. Squeeze out a little paste.

2 For grass, trim off the paste from the end of the sugarcraft gun with the back of a craft knife. Attach the trimmed off 'grass' to your project.

3 For hair on a character, hold the sugarcraft gun near the head. Add sugar glue to the head and trim against the head with the back of a craft knife so the hair sticks.

4 Here is the trimmed hair on the head.

Flared flower

You will need

Modelling paste or flower/petal paste
5-petal cutter
Flower pad
Large ball tool
Sugar glue
Foam drying sheet
Large daisy-centre stamp

1 Roll out the modelling paste or flower/petal paste until it is paper thin. Cut out 3 flowers.

2 Put a flower on a flower pad and use the large ball tool to soften the edges to flare them.

3 Flare all the petals on all of the flowers.

4 Glue all your flowers together, overlapping them so you can see all the petals to form a well-shaped flower.

5 Set the flowers on the foam drying sheet to dry.

6 Roll three small balls of paste and stamp them with a large daisy-centre stamp to make a centre for each flower.

7 Add the flower centre before the flower dries.

8 Leave the flower overnight so that it sets properly and holds its shape.

Cutter and veiner sets

You will need
Modelling paste
Rolling pin
Cutter and veiner set
Foam drying sheet
Sugar pearl

1 Roll out the modelling paste.

2 Cut out a flower from the paste.

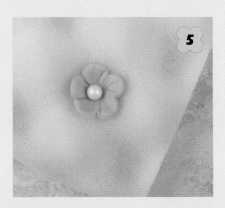

3 Put the flower onto the veiner on the side that is indented. Close the veiner to imprint on the flower.

4 Put the flower onto the foam drying sheet.

5 Add the green sugar pearl before the icing dries.

Quick and easy leaf

You will need
Green sugarpaste, flower/petal paste
  or modelling paste
Heart cutter

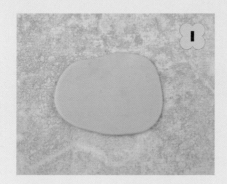

1 Roll out some green icing from sugarpaste, flower paste or modelling paste, ensuring it is even.

2 Cut out a heart in the size of your choice.

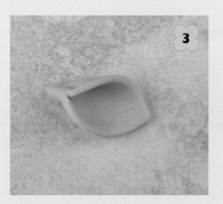

3 Fold the rounded parts of the heart inwards to shape the leaf.

Templates

1½in (3.5cm)

⅞in (2cm)

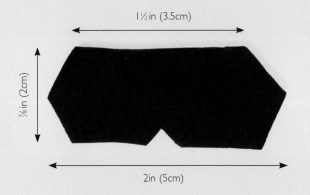

2in (5cm)

Mini pirate (page 46) waistcoat template
(approximate sizes)

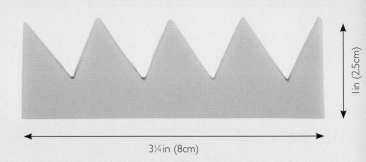

1in (2.5cm)

3¼in (8cm)

Princess crown (page 70) template
(approximate sizes)

About the author

Shereen van Ballegooyen was born in Zimbabwe but grew up in South Africa. She moved to the UK with her husband in 2001 and they now live in Hertfordshire with their two young daughters.

The first birthday cake Shereen made for her oldest daughter in 2007 was a messy, buttercream-covered penguin-shaped cake. With practice and encouragement from friends Shereen had soon caught the cake-making bug and in 2009 she was asked to make her first paid-for cake. Before long Shereen was able to start her own cake business, which continues to thrive.

Shereen is completely self-taught, having found the internet and books to be a great source of information. She has found the best way of learning to be through good old trial and error, helped by the fact that she adores what she does.

She started to publicize her work through a Facebook group, Shereen's Cakes & Bakes in 2011, and the page has gone from strength to strength. Her online tutorials proved very popular, which is what inspired her to write this book.

www.facebook.com/shereenscakesandbakesstevenage

Acknowledgements from Shereen

A very big thank you to my friend Sarah Oxborough in Australia, who bought me my very first decorating book – *Cakes to Inspire and Desire* by Lindy Smith. Sarah encouraged me to cover my cakes with sugarpaste and to start making decorations.

Vanessa Iti from Bella Cupcakes, based in New Zealand, remains my greatest inspiration. I learned from her that cupcakes definitely require more than just a buttercream swirl and a flower!

And I wouldn't have got this far without incredible support, honesty and love from my husband and my family and friends. They all encouraged me from the start and continue to support me every step of the way.

Suppliers

AUSTRALIA

Bake Boss
359–361 Swan Street
Richmond, Victoria 3121
Tel: +613 9429 2116
www.bakeboss.com.au

Baking Pleasures
www.bakingpleasures.com.au

Cake Decorating Central
Unit 2/5 Harbord Road
Woodbine, New South Wales 2568
Tel: +612 9899 3065
www.cakedecoratingcentral.com

Cakes Around Town
Unit 2/12 Sudbury Street
Darra, Brisbane QLD 4076
Tel: +617 3160 8728
www.cakesaroundtown.com.au

CANADA

Flour Confections
1084 Brock (Salk) Rd Unit 5
401/Brock Court
Pickering, Ontario, L1W 4B6
Tel: +1 905 492 2692
www.flourconfections.com

IRELAND

Bakeworld
St Cuan, Ballybrennan, Bree
County Wexford
Tel: +353 053 924 7362
www.bakeworld.ie

Stuff 4 Cakes
Cloonboo, Currandulla
County Galway
Tel: +353 087 756 5148
www.stuff4cakes.ie

NEW ZEALAND

The Cake Shop
PO Box 1209, Pukekohe, Auckland
New Zealand
www.thecakeshop.co.nz

Cake Stuff
322 Heretaunga Street West
Hastings
Tel: +64 6 870 3172
www.cakestuff.co.nz

Kiwi Cake Supplies
PO Box 4441, Kamo, Whangarei
0141, Northland
www.kiwicakes.co.nz

Sugarcrafts
99 Queens Road
Panmure, Auckland 1072
Tel: +64 9 527 6060
www.sugarcrafts.co.nz

SINGAPORE

Bake it yourself – Singapore
182 Bukit Timah Road
Singapore 229853
www.b-i-y.com

SOUTH AFRICA

Bakels
235 Main Road, Martindale
Johannesburg, Gauteng 2000
Tel: +27 11 673 2100
www.sbakels.co.za

UK

BAKO London & South East
Units 1–6, Merton Industrial Park
Lee Road, London SW19 3XX
Tel: +44 (0)20 8543 1212
www.callbakolondon.com

Cake Craft World
7 Chatterton Road, Bromley
Kent BR2 9QW
Tel: +44 (0)1732 46 35 73
www.cakecraftworld.co.uk

The Cake Decorating Company
Shop 2B Triumph Road
Nottingham NG7 2GA
Tel: +44 (0)1158 224521
www.thecakedecoratingcompany.co.uk

Cakes, Cookies & Crafts
Unit 2, Francis Business Park
White Lund Industrial Estate
Morecambe, Lancashire LA3 3PT
Tel: +44 (0)1524 389684
www.cakescookiesandcraftsshop.co.uk

Party Animal Online
10–11 Evans Business Park
Amy Johnson Way, Blackpool
Lancashire FY4 2RF
Tel: +44(0)1253 408708
www.partyanimalonlineshop.com

Pretty Witty Cakes
Rannoch Road, Crowborough
East Sussex TN6 1RB
or +44 (0)1892 611710
www.prettywittycakes.co.uk

USA

Cake Supplies Depot
1379 S. University Drive, Plantation,
Florida 33324
Tel: +1 954 472 2700
www.cakesuppliesdepot.com

CalJava Online
Tel: +1 818 718 2707
www.caljavaonline.com

Decopac
3500 Thurston Avenue
Anoka, Minnesota 55303
www.decopac.com

Fondant Source
Cake & Craft llc
1205 E. Donegan Ave
Kissimmee, Florida 34744
www.fondantsource.com

Global Sugar Art
625 Route 3, Unit 3
Plattsburgh, New York 12901
Tel: +1 518 561 3039
www.globalsugarart.com

**Kerekes Bakery &
Restaurant Equipment Inc.**
6103 15th Avenue
Brooklyn, New York 11219
Tel: +1 718 232 7044
www.bakedeco.com

Kitchen Krafts
PO Box 442
Waukon, Iowa 52172-0442
Tel: +1 563 535 8000
www.kitchenkrafts.com

Lucks Food Decorating Company
3003 S. Pine St
Tacoma, Washington 98409-4713
www.lucks.com

Sugar Delites
405 E. Kott Rd
Manistee, Michigan 49660
Tel: +1 231 723 5774
www.jenniferdontz.com

Index

Names of projects shown in italics

To order a book, or to request a catalogue, contact:
GMC Publications Ltd
Castle Place, 166 High Street, Lewes, East Sussex, BN7 IXU
United Kingdom
Tel: +44 (0)1273 488005 **Website:** www.gmcbooks.com